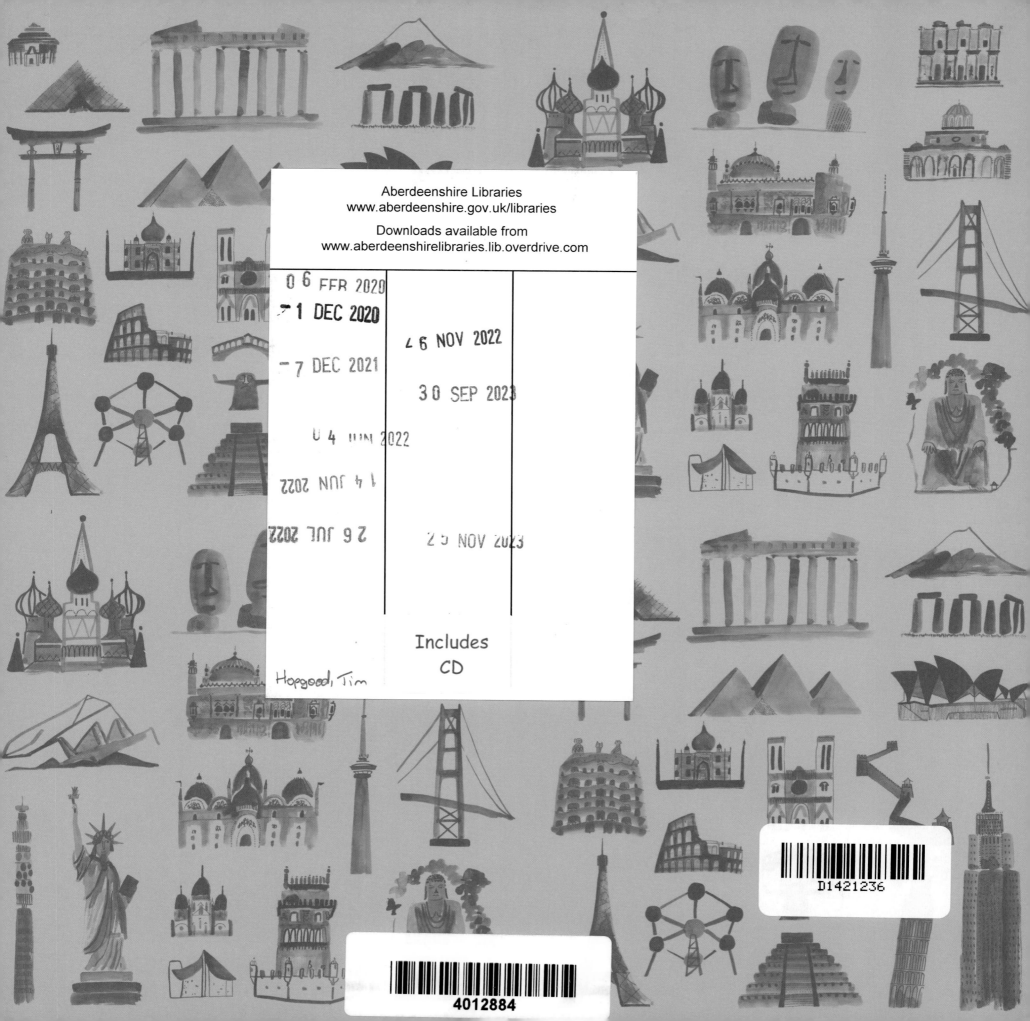

Includes
CD

This book belongs to:

. . . .

for all the day-dreamers of this **WORLD X**

OXFORD
UNIVERSITY PRESS

Great Clarendon Street, Oxford OX2 6DP

Oxford University Press is a department of the University of Oxford.
It furthers the University's objective of excellence in research, scholarship,
and education by publishing worldwide. Oxford is a registered trade mark
of Oxford University Press in the UK and in certain other countries

'Moon River' Words and Music by Henry Mancini and Johnny Mercer © 1960
Reproduced by permission of Sony/ATV Harmony, London W1F 9LD
Illustrations © Tim Hopgood 2018

The moral rights of the author have been asserted

Database right Oxford University Press (maker)

First published 2018

British Library Cataloguing in Publication Data
Data available

ISBN: 978-0-19-274639-9 (hardback with CD)
ISBN: 978-0-19-274640-5 (paperback with CD)

10 9 8 7 6 5 4 3 2 1

Printed in China

Paper used in the production of this book is a natural, recyclable product
made from wood grown in sustainable forests. The manufacturing process
conforms to the environmental regulations of the country of origin.

PICTURES BY

tim hopgood

MOON RIVER

BASED ON THE SONG BY JOHNNY MERCER & HENRY MANCINI

OXFORD

UNIVERSITY PRESS

Moon River, wider than a mile,
I'm crossing you in style some day.

Oh, **dream maker,** you heart breaker.

Wherever you're going, I'm going your way.

Two drifters,
off to see the world.

There's such a **lot of world** to see.

We're after the same

rainbow's end...

. . . waiting round the bend.

My **huckleberry** friend,
moon river, and me.

Moon river,
wider than a mile,

I'm crossing you
in style some day.

Oh, dream maker,
you heart breaker.

. . . I'm going your way.

Two drifters,
off to see the world.

There's such a lot

We're
after
the
same . . .

rainbow's end . . .

. . . waiting round
        the bend.

My huckleberry friend,

moon river, and me.

MOON RIVER

BASED ON THE SONG BY
JOHNNY MERCER & HENRY MANCINI

Moon River, wider than a mile,
I'm crossing you in style some day.

Oh, dream maker, you heart breaker.
Wherever you're going, I'm going your way.

Two drifters, off to see the world.
There's such a lot of world to see!

We're after the same rainbow's end,
waiting round the bend.

My huckleberry friend, moon river, and me.

Moon River, wider than a mile,
I'm crossing you in style some day.

Oh, dream maker, you heart breaker.
Wherever you're going, I'm going your way.

Two drifters, off to see the world.
There's such a lot of world to see!

We're after the same rainbow's end,
waiting round the bend.

My huckleberry friend, moon river, and me.

I can't think of a better song to drift off to sleep to than Moon River.
It's a song full of adventure and big dreams. Stepping out into the unknown
can seem scary, but instead of fear there is a powerful sense of hope running
through the song, like the wide river itself, which keeps on flowing.

The joy of discovering new places and meeting new faces helps us to look at
the world with fresh eyes. As we make our way through life, it's the friendships
that we make and the dreams that we share along the way that make life's
journey so worthwhile.

Sweet dreams.

timhopgood